JEWISH HOLIDAY & SABBATH JOURNAL

By Edward Hoffman, Ph.D.

CHRONICLE BOOKS
SAN FRANCISCO

10 9 8 7 6 5 4 3 2 1

Printed in China

Distributed in Canada by
Raincoast Books
9050 Shaughnessy Street
Vancouver, B.C. V6P 6E5

Chronicle Books LLC
85 Second Street
San Francisco, CA 94105
www.chroniclebooks.com

Design by Ph.D

ISBN: 0-8118-3303-8

To Aaron and Jeremy

RELATED WORKS BY EDWARD HOFFMAN

Jewish Wisdom: A Journal

Opening the Inner Gates: New Paths in Kabbalah and Psychology

Sparks of Light: Counseling in the Hasidic Tradition

The Heavenly Ladder: A Kabbalistic Guide to Inner Growth

The Hebrew Alphabet: A Mystical Journey

The Kabbalah Deck

The Way of Splendor: Jewish Mysticism and Modern Psychology

Acknowledgments

This project would scarcely have been completed if it were not for the valuable help of others. I'm grateful to Debra Lande, Executive Editor at Chronicle Books, for her initial and sustained enthusiasm throughout my effort. It's been truly delightful working with her. Editorial assistant Carey Jones has been consistently helpful. I'm also indebted to editor Alan Rapp for first introducing my Judaica work several years ago to his colleagues at Chronicle Books.

I wish to thank Sara Axel, Dr. Gerald Epstein, Cantor Bruce Halev, Aaron Hostyk, Rabbi Neal Kaunfer, Paul Palnik, Rabbi Steve Rosman, and Rabbi Rami Shapiro for their many stimulating conversations. Their encouragement, warmth, and insights are very much appreciated.

To all of the above, as well as to my Judaica teachers and students over the years—and to my family—I wish to offer thanks and the hope that this project will enhance our celebration of Jewish life throughout the year.

Contents

Introduction

Precious moments, sacred moments. As Jews, we're empowered throughout the year—and on every Sabbath and new moon—to experience the divine amidst the everyday world. Together with Torah study during millennia of history, our cycle of *Shabbat* and holiday celebrations has sustained Judaism as both a religion and a way of life.

As members of families, local communities, and the Jewish people as a whole, including those who have converted to Judaism, our personal observance of holiday rituals, customs, and prayerful gatherings links us to others, and to our forebears. Certainly, our deeply-held tradition of social compassion and justice emanates from such communal involvement. In addition, the mystical traditions of the Kabbalah and early Hasidism have imbued these celebrations with renewed spirit.

In our celebrations and commemorations, we take our cue from the classic dictum of the Passover *Haggadah,* the prayerbook of the *seder* (ritual meal): "All Jews, in all generations, should celebrate as though they had personally been liberated from Egypt." Our later sages emphasized that every Jewish holy day speaks to us individually as well as collectively, guiding us in family life and relationship, health, and livelihood. Thus, Passover not only commemorates the Israelites' liberation from Egyptian bondage, but also inspires us to overcome the pressures of our workaday routine that enslave and stifle our full potential. Similarly, the festival of *Sukkot* doesn't just reenact the saga of the Israelites who lived in desert huts after fleeing Egypt. It symbolically reminds every Jew to become less attached to property and possessions in life's spiritual journey.

Today there is a growing interest in relating the Jewish festivals to personal spirituality. To this end, I've created the *Jewish Holiday & Sabbath Journal*, designed to strengthen your awareness and connection with the Sabbath, the monthly new moon festival called *Rosh Hodesh* (literally "Head of the Month" in Hebrew), and the major holidays. Because of my focus on renewing tradition, I've necessarily omitted the two modern Jewish holidays of *Yom HaShoah* (Holocaust Memorial Day) and *Yom HaAtzmaut* (Israel Independence Day). Likewise, in honoring tradition, my emphasis is threefold, encompassing learning, activity, and self-reflection.

This book begins with Sabbath and *Rosh Hodesh*, the most frequently occurring Jewish holidays. Then, starting with *Rosh Hashanah* ("Head of the Year"), the next eleven chapters follow the holidays' temporal order in the Hebrew calendar. Every chapter begins with a brief overview of history and ritual, and then offers specific suggestions for guided activities based on the holiday's themes.

For instance, *Rosh Hashanah* as the Jewish New Year focuses on repentance (more broadly known as *teshuvah* in Hebrew) and spiritual rebirth. In recognition of Judaism's focus on relationship as vital to spiritual well-being, I invite you on *Rosh Hashanah* to identify a new, uplifting friendship or family tie that you experienced during the past Hebrew year—and then make a celebratory New Year's card—to send to that person.

To commemorate *Hanukkah* more personally, I encourage you to build your own *hanukkiyah* (*Hanukkah menorah*) with a companion. In this way, we become linked strongly not only to past generations of Jews, but also to our children, grandchildren, and even our unborn descendants. These celebrations and activities tranform us into a living bridge spanning ancient sacred times and reaching to a redemptive future of global peace and enlightenment.

Each chapter ends with a "Reflections" section, providing space to record your favorite memories—as well as musings, plans, and dreams awakened by that holiday; the Torah authorizes such writing after *Shabbat*'s weekly completion and after particular holy days. As we get older, such memories become more beautiful. For instance, my brother, Barry, and I will always fondly remember how as children, we would bet each other who would be the first Passover guest to spill a wine cup accidentally at the crowded *seder* dinner table (it was almost always our Russian-born grandma Ida.) You may not have such an endearing family memory for *Shavuot*, which celebrates the revelatory giving of the Torah to the Jews at Mount Sinai. Nonetheless, this spring holiday offers an excellent time to reflect on the revelations and spiritual lessons of your own life, and this journal enables you to record your thoughts.

Within our millennia-old tradition, such holiday-related writing is the very essence of Jewishness. Keeping a journal to narrate personal experience has long been part of our cultural heritage, sustaining our popular appellation as "People of the Book." As the Baal Shem Tov, founder of Hasidism aptly declared, "Forgetfulness is exile. Remembrance is redemption."

At the end of this journal, you'll also find a glossary that explains all the italicized Hebrew words, and a resources section to guide future study.

Judaism has been called a divine gift. Whether it heightens your appreciation for past good times and family fun and festivity, deepens your interest in sacred study, or helps to guide your inner growth, the *Jewish Holiday & Sabbath Journal* is offered in this perennial spirit. It's my hope that this innovative journal format will especially provide new impetus and inspiration on your spiritual journey throughout the Hebrew year.

HEBREW ALPHABET (ALEFBET)

He (H) **Dalet** (D) **Gimel** (G) **Bet** (B/V) **Alef** (silent)

Yod (Y) **Tet** (T) **Chet** (Ch) **Zayin** (Z) **Vav** (V/O/U)

Samech (S) **Nun** (N) **Mem** (M) **Lamed** (L) **Kaf** (K/Kh)

Resh (R) **Qof** (Q) **Tzade** (Tz) **Pe** (P/F) **Ayin** (silent)

Tav (T/S) **Shin** (Sh/S)

Sabbath

Ushered in with the lighting of candles, Sabbath, or *Shabbat*, brings God's radiance and delight into every week of our Jewish lives. Celebrated from sundown Friday to sundown Saturday, it's the only festival that's part of the Ten Commandments given to Jews at Mount Sinai. For millennia, Sabbath celebration has been perhaps the most vibrant and fundamental feature of Jewish life. In the Talmud's memorable maxim, "Even more than the Jews have kept *Shabbat*, *Shabbat* has kept the Jews."

Unlike other Jewish holidays, the Sabbath marks neither a seasonal harvest nor a definable historical event. Nor does the Sabbath depend on the lunar cycle. According to the sages, this holy day existed mysteriously even before the Act of Creation. When we observe and honor its presence each week, our soul flourishes. As the modern rabbinic thinker Abraham Joshua Heschel declared poetically, "The meaning of the Sabbath is to celebrate time rather than space. Six days a week, we live under the tyranny of things of space; on the Sabbath, we try to become attuned to *holiness in time*."

"For six days you shall do your work," proclaims the Fourth Commandment, "but the seventh day is for you a day of rest." However, that day of rest doesn't just happen automatically. Maintaining a day of holiness involves considerable preparation and guideposts. That's why a myriad of religious dicta or *mitzvot*—never mentioned at all in the Bible—arose over many centuries. The rabbis developed a series of prohibitions against such everyday activities as writing or weaving, conducting business or farming, sewing, hammering, journeying, lighting fires or cooking, and even tearing paper or tying permanent knots. In the rabbinic view, the purpose of these *mitzvot* is to "safeguard" *Shabbat* from being debased and demeaned into an ordinary workday. In the face of our current, technologically driven "24/7" view of commerce, the sages of old seemed to have had uncanny prescience.

Shabbat, like most Jewish holidays, isn't celebrated simply by going to synagogue. Instead, holiness begins at home, with candle-lighting before sunset on Friday evening, followed by *kiddush* (blessing over wine), and the blessing over freshly baked braided bread (*hallah*), followed by a festive meal. The next morning, Jews read from the Torah at synagogue, returning home for a special Shabbat luncheon.

The day of rest concludes with a worship service known as *havdalah* ("separation" in Hebrew). In recent years, these rituals, which infuse the return to the everyday world with the sweetness of holy time, are providing renewed inspiration for many Jews. Marked by singing and gathering in a circle, *havdalah* rituals include lighting a braided candle, dousing the flame in a cup of wine, and inhaling fragrant spices.

Shabbat also has a mystical side. During the sixteenth century in the Land of Israel, leading Kabbalists (practitioners of Jewish mysticism) developed rituals centering on *Shabbat's* transcendent holiness. Every Sabbath morning, Rabbi Isaac Luria and his followers would form a procession and move out to the surrounding fields. Wearing white flowing garments, they would wait to receive the spirit of the *Shekhinah* or "Sabbath Queen," whose presence personified this sacred day. They would welcome this divine presence with the song *Lekha Dodi* ("Come, My Beloved"), still part of Jewish liturgy around the world today.

Consistent with the ancient belief that the soul is exalted by *Shabbat's* unique spiritual power, Rabbi Luria and other Safed Kabbalists, as well as later Hasidic leaders, would typically speak on this day about the hidden reaches of human consciousness and the cosmos. Today the Sabbath's transcendent power is stimulating many Jews to meditate and study mystical texts on this holy day.

How can you optimize *Shabbat's* vibrancy in your life? There are two key aspects: celebrating each Sabbath more fully, and integrating its sacred qualities better into the secular week. By tradition, the first dimension extols prayer and prescribed ritual. The second, perhaps more challenging in today's work-dominated society, encompasses a variety of methods, including journal-keeping, sacred study, and regular meditative practice. As the Hasidic master Rabbi Nachman of Bratslav advised, "The joy of *Shabbat* is really the gateway to true freedom. Through it, you can reach the highest levels. Be careful to feel nothing but joy on *Shabbat*, for nothing compares with its greatness and holiness."

RECOMMENDED ACTIVITIES

Savor a delicious meal that you've prepared or cooked before Sabbath. Allow yourself ample time. With sensual delight, taste each morsel fully. To enhance your sense of personal renewal, make something special, different. To lighten the workload and share the joy, invite friends and family to participate in the cooking and preparation. Many people enjoy getting together in *havurot* (study groups or friendship circles) to share not only the meal of *Shabbat*, but Hebrew or Yiddish songs, discussions of the week's Torah portion, and Hasidic or inspirational stories.

Sit in a relaxed position, and free yourself from distractions. Think about the week that's just ended, and identify a blessing that you experienced: an act of kindness, an encouraging word, a moment of joy. Now express gratitude to the Holy One. Next, think about the coming week and plan a good deed (*mitzvah*) for someone in your life. Let it be unexpected, a surprise. Encourage others to identify these blessings and perform *mitzvot*.

This is the best day of the week to practice Jewish meditation. If you're a beginner, an excellent technique involves the Hebrew letters. (See page 13.) Each Sabbath, focus on a particular letter, its meaning and spiritual relevance for your life.

Because holy time requires preparation, get others involved, particularly children. If you have time, try baking *hallah* at home with children or friends. Give children pieces of dough to bake their own mini-*challot*. Following the commandment in Deuteronomy to "teach your children well," tell them about the significance of *Shabbat* and each of the blessings: candles, wine, bread, and the *Birkhat Hamazon*, the blessing after the meal. Invite them to help decorate the table, perhaps using ritual objects or craft items they have made. Invite them to do the *Motzi*, the blessing, said over the bread.

Invite friends for a *havdalah* gathering. Begin with the ceremonies, perhaps outdoors under the stars, and then move on to singing or Israeli dancing, or perhaps discussing a Jewish book.

Take a long, leisurely walk, with family or with a companion. Walk for at least an hour, and feel the spiritual vibrancy of your "Sabbath soul" and the *Shekhinah's* presence accompanying you.

REFLECTIONS

Rosh Hodesh

Rosh Hodesh (which literally means the "Head of the Month") involves personal and communal renewal. It's a time to become more receptive to our souls' hidden, dreamy, visionary side. An ancient holiday that celebrated the appearance of the new moon to mark the new Hebrew month, *Rosh Hodesh* lapsed into obscurity for most of the modern era. Outside of Hasidism, it was ignored almost completely.

But in recent years, especially among women eager to forge a renewed Jewish spiritual identity, the monthly festival has gained increasing importance. Drawing upon folklore and historical ritual, women rabbis and theologians, as well as those who are reconnecting to Judaism, are reclaiming the moon as a classic Jewish symbol of feminine creativity and transformation.

Rosh Hodesh is also a monthly holiday for women, liberating them from some of their traditional tasks. Historically, Jewish women observed *Rosh Hodesh* by refraining from spinning, sewing, weaving, or needlework. For some women today, *Rosh Hodesh*, with its lunar focus, also relates to water, the tides, and the monthly menstrual cycle.

In recent years, Jewish women have been getting together at *Rosh Hodesh* to share insights about Judaism, womanhood, and the divine. It's become an honored time for candle-lighting, story-telling, studying Torah, and meditating for spiritual growth and harmony. This phenomenon of re-shaping an age-old holiday and giving it renewed relevance for contemporary Jewish life has been a vibrant feature of Judaism for millennia.

In ancient Judaism, before a new month could be declared, the guardians of Jewish law had to confirm the birth of the new moon, defined as the first visible sliver of light after the old moon had faded completely. During the Temple epoch, calculating the calendar was one of the chief duties of the *Sanhedrin*, the seventy-one-member Jewish high court in Jerusalem. The determination of the holy days depended on them.

How did they know when the new month began? On the 30th day of each month, the *Sanhedrin* would convene and wait for testimony from witnesses who had seen the new moon's light. If the judges determined that at least two witnesses were reliable, they'd declare that the new month had begun. A *shofar* (ram's horn) was then blown, and bonfires would be lit from mountaintop to mountaintop in visible proclamation.

In the biblical era, *Rosh Hodesh* was observed by feasting, and women particularly would seek out the prophets for guidance. Much later, in the sixteenth century, Kabbalists in the Holy Land town of Safed celebrated *Rosh Hodesh* as a small *Yom Kippur*, a day of fasting and deep meditation.

The Safed Kabbalists also instituted the ritual of blessing the new moon in a ceremony on the first or second Sabbath night each month. Known as *kiddush levana* (hallowing the moon), this ritual is always performed outdoors and only if the moon can actually be seen.

The Sabbath before the new moon is known as Sabbath *Mevorchim* ("Blessing"). After the Torah reading, the congregation rises and the cantor or other designated prayer-leader chants a special blessing:

"God, grant us a long and peaceful life,

A life of goodness and blessing,

A life of achievement and strength of body,

A life of decency and dignity, free from shame and full of honor,

A life filled with Torah and love for You."

Then a proclamation is made, announcing when the new moon will appear, to the exact hour. To reinforce this news, congregants repeat the proclamation. When *Rosh Hodesh* falls on a Sabbath, Numbers 28:9–15 is read in the synagogue, along with the regular weekly Torah portion and a special *haftarah*, Isaiah 66:1–24, which bespeaks of hope and Jewish rebirth.

Because *Rosh Hodesh* is always celebrated as a day of joy, Psalms 113–118, which convey a mood of praise and rejoicing, are recited. These psalms are known collectively as *Hallel, a name* derived from *halleluyah*, the very first word in Psalm 113; it means "praise God."

Rosh Hodesh offers light on the tides and wellsprings of the soul—especially those currents that provide vitality and replenishment in everyday life. In the inspiring words of the *Zohar* (Judaism's primary mystical text), "Just as the celestial stream flows on forever without ceasing, so one must see that his own river and spring shall not cease in the world."

RECOMMENDED ACTIVITIES

Think of a meaningful dream you've had in the past month, either while you were sleeping or daydreaming. Draw a corresponding picture or create a collage that reminds you of the dream. After you've done so, display it in your home until the next Rosh Hodesh. Invite others in your household, including children, to also draw pictures and share their stories about them.

Identify a blessing—such as a new person, joyful event, or uplifting experience—that came into your life during the past month. Say the *Shehechiyanu* (see the Glossary) aloud as an expression of gratitude.

Plan a good deed (*mitzvah*), such as an unexpected gift or event, for someone between now and the next *Rosh Hodesh*. Make your plan as thorough as possible, and share it with two others to elicit their additional suggestions. Then perform the *mitzvah*.

Draw a picture of the moon in whatever phase you find most appealing. The traditional Hebrew word for moon is *yaraiach*, which begins with a *yud*. Draw a colorful letter *yud* in honor of the moon. When you've finished your picture, display it in your home until the next *Rosh Hodesh*. Again, if you have children or grandchildren, get them to draw pictures of the moon and tell stories or write poems above it.

Start a Rosh Hodesh group, inviting women to come together for singing, meditation, storytelling, or art that touches on the experiences of women in Judaism. Share foods in the shape of the moon, such as cookies, eggs, or bagels.

Take a walk outside, weather permitting, to witness the different phases of the moon.

Create a lovely centerpiece with candles or flowers to inspire meditation on Rosh Hodesh.

REFLECTIONS

Rosh Hashanah

Rosh Hashanah, literally the "Head of the Year," marks a new beginning, a time of *teshuvah*. Often mistranslated simply as repentance, this Hebrew word has a more precise meaning: returning to our inner source of holiness and transcendence. In Jewish tradition, *teshuvah* during the Days of Awe (the ten-day period encompassing *Rosh Hashanah* and *Yom Kippur*) is a dynamic process involving self-examination and intentionality (*kavana*). We aim to change for the better in our relations with others, with our own highest nature, and with God as revealed in the Torah. Indeed, this holiday, falling at the start of a new fall season, feels more like a time of new beginnings than the secular holiday celebrated on January 1.

In the Bible, the festival is identified in Leviticus 23:32: "In the seventh month [that is, *Tishri*], on the first day of the month, there shall be a solemn rest for you, a sacred convocation commemorated with the blast of the *shofar*. You shall not work at your ordinary labor, and you shall bring a fire-offering to the Lord."

The Torah identifies the festival as *Yom Teruah* (the Day of Sounding the *Shofar*) or *Yom Hazikkaron* (the Day of Remembering). Not until the Talmudic era, millennia later, was this day called *Rosh Hashanah*, or the New Year. Scholars today believe that after the First Temple of Jerusalem was destroyed in 586 B.C.E., and the Jewish people had become enslaved by Babylon, the 1st of *Tishri* acquired new meaning as a time for self-reflection about Jewish purpose and affirmation, and becoming "inscribed in the Book of Life."

The entire preceding month of *Elul* is a time of preparation for the Days of Awe. The *shofar* is blown after every morning service, and Jews greet one another and send cards or e-mails with the message *Shanah tovah* ("a good year") or *Le-shanah tovah tikatevu* ("May you be inscribed for a good year in the Book of Life"). It's also customary to visit the gravesites of loved ones during *Elul*.

The only special biblical ritual for *Rosh Hashanah* is the blowing of the *shofar*. For many centuries, the sages have interpreted its eerie, untuned, and powerfully soul-wrenching sound as a cry to awaken our sleeping souls into purposeful action and *teshuvah*. The *shofar* is blown in three ways: *tekiah*, one long blast of alarm; *shevarim,* three medium blasts that sound like wailing; and *teruah*, nine short blasts like broken sobs.

Called "the birthday of the world," *Rosh Hashanah* reminds us of God's creation of the cosmos at the beginning of time. Yet the designated Torah reading isn't the Genesis 1 story of creation, but the birth of Isaac to aged Sarah and Abraham in Genesis 21. Why? Because in Judaism, each human is regarded as a miniature universe, and the birth of a child, especially to parents late in life, is truly a celebratory event. For Jews, too, *Rosh Hashanah*, represents a time of new life and renewal, reflected in Sarah's miraculous pregnancy.

On the first afternoon of *Rosh Hashanah*, if it doesn't fall on *Shabbat*, Jews traditionally walk to the nearest body of flowing water (a river, lake, or ocean) and symbolically cast sins away by throwing in bread crumbs. The ancient ceremony is known in Hebrew as *tashlikh* ("casting"), and involves reciting Micah 7:18–20, Psalms 118:5–9, and Psalms 33 and 130. It takes its name from the verse in Micah, "You will cast [*tashlikh*] your sins into the depths of the sea."

In addition to lighting candles and saying *kiddush*, which are part of all Jewish holidays, our home celebrations incorporate several food customs. Jews dip apples or other foods, such as *hallah*, in honey to express the desire for a sweet year.

As we dip, we recite the phrase, "May it be Your will to renew us for a year that is good and sweet!" In addition, the *hallah* at *Rosh Hashanah* is round in shape and sometimes sweetened with raisins; the roundness symbolizes the wholeness of the world and a new beginning, while the raisins echo the theme of sweetness. Honey cake is a traditional treat. At this time of year, we partake of fruit we've not tasted for a long period of time, to augment our sense of personal renewal, and avoid nuts (since the corresponding Hebrew word, *egoz*, has the same numerical equivalent as that for *chet*, meaning sin).

Though every Jewish holiday in its own way asks that we stretch and grow spiritually, *Rosh Hashanah* more than any other emphasizes our personal relationship with God. Now is the time to plan how to correct your spiritual weaknesses, such as anger or impatience, as well as accent your undeveloped strengths. As the late Lubavitcher leader Rabbi Menachem Schneerson, aptly declared, "*Teshuvah* does not involve creating anything new, but rediscovering the goodness that was always there."

RECOMMENDED ACTIVITIES

Make a "wish picture" collage showing what you'd like to see manifested in your life during the coming year. Then make one for a friend or family member, after getting their input. Your collage should reflect "soulful" themes, not just materialistic desires. Or do this as an activity with friends and family members.

Invite your children to change something in their rooms. This is a good time to do a *mitzvah* by giving away the toys or clothing that they have outgrown and perhaps adding a new element that reflects where they are now.

Share the *tashlikh* ceremony with a buddy or a family member. Talk about the "flaw" or shortcoming that you would like to discard this year and what steps you are going to take to accomplish it. Talk about the positive things you are going to do to transform yourself. Then check in with your buddy periodically throughout the new year to see how you are doing.

Reflecting on the past Hebrew year, write about something new and uplifting that involved someone in your life: the birth or growth of a friendship, a shared activity or trip, perhaps a long-awaited reconciliation. Then, make a card to celebrate this event and send it to that person.

Plan to do something utterly new and different in the ten special days between *Rosh Hashanah* and *Yom Kippur*, such as visiting a place you've never been before. If you're not sure what to do, ask a friend or family member to suggest something unusual but appropriate for you. Then follow their suggestion.

During the High Holy Days, contribute nonperishable items to a food bank, make a donation to a charity that feeds the hungry, or help out at a soup kitchen. Volunteering in this way can be more rewarding when you do it with friends, family, or fellow congregants.

Change something in your home. This can be a major renovation or a simpler re-arrangement of furniture and interior design. The important thing is that you consciously make a change to improve your home's ambience in a way you find appealing.

Make *Shanah tovah* cards with family members or friends, cutting out pictures from magazines that symbolize new beginnings for them.

REFLECTIONS

Yom Kippur

Yom Kippur ("Day of Atonement") is about forgiveness: forgiving others for the wrongs they may have committed in our lives, seeking others' forgiveness for our own shortcomings, and seeking God's forgiveness as well. Jews traditionally observe *Yom Kippur* as the most important day of the Hebrew calendar for intense self-reflection: Why are we here? What does it mean to be alive in the few decades that mark human existence? What is our Jewish soul meant to accomplish on earth? And how can we better fulfill this mission in the new year that has just begun?

Yom Kippur is mandated in the Pentateuch (known in Jewish tradition as the Five Books of Moses). According to Leviticus 23:26–28, the Lord tells Moses, "On the tenth day of the seventh month you shall afflict your souls and do no work. For on this day atonement shall be made for you to cleanse you. Before God, you shall be cleansed of all your sins."

Clarifying *Yom Kippur*'s meaning for all Jewry, the eleventh-century sage Maimonides commented, "It is the day of repentance for all, for the individual and for the community. It is the time of pardon and forgiveness for Israel. Therefore, everyone is obligated to repent and confess wrongdoing."

Originally, *Yom Kippur* involved special rituals conducted by the high priest in the First Temple of Jerusalem, built in approximately 960 B.C.E. A bull and goat were sacrificed, and a second goat was sent away into the wilderness in a mysterious ceremony to honor "Azazel," possibly a desert spirit, no longer known today.

By the time of the Second Temple of Jerusalem, built in approximately 516 C.E., the high priest also appeared before the people on *Yom Kippur* and recited a confessional plea three times: first for his own wrongdoing and that of his household, second for the Levi (priestly) tribe, and third for the entire Jewish people.

On this holiday alone, the high priest would enter the "Holy of Holies"—the Temple's most sacred chamber—and utter aloud a secret name of God, whose pronunciation is no longer known. That name, which God is said to have uttered to Moses at the burning bush, was then transmitted orally by Jewish leaders through the generations. The purpose of the high priest's ritual was to implore divine protection.

After the Second Temple was destroyed in 70 C.E., ending much of the ancient Jews' communal rituals, *Yom Kippur* gained even greater importance because of its emphasis on the individual's relationship to God. In rabbinical eyes, the sacred day brought Jews closer to heavenly realms, the angels, and "Jerusalem on High" than any other day in the Hebrew calendar.

Yom Kippur is the better known of Judaism's two major fast days (the other is *Tisha B'Av*, in the summer). Its mood is set by the inspiring *Kol Nidre* evening service, said to have been instituted in the thirteenth century so that those who had violated communal regulations could return to the community. The *Kol Nidre* prayer, along with the confession of sins, became integral to *Yom Kippur*, for the rabbis saw its applicability to all Jews seeking to recognize and rectify their shortcomings.

On this day of spiritual cleansing and purification, many Jews dress in white. Besides refraining from eating, drinking, and bathing, Jews traditionally remove their leather shoes and put on cloth ones, since leather has been deemed a luxury, too fancy for this day's somber mood. Moreover, wearing animal skins is viewed as akin to consuming meat, out of keeping with the fast day.

Yom Kippur empowers us to focus on life's most serious and important questions. Fasting and heartfelt prayer are time-honored tools that help in this process. In comparison to other Jewish holidays, it is somber and serious. Like the prophet Jonah (whose biblical book is read in the synagogue on *Yom Kippur*), we each have a mission on earth for an allotted period of time. Our dedication, intentionality, and spiritual sensitivity are instruments for achieving it. Now is the time to meditate about our mission and how to best involve others in our life's momentous voyage.

RECOMMENDED ACTIVITIES

Hasidism teaches that we're all like Jonah, who hears a divine calling but tries to ignore it. Name a skill you'd like to learn this year, such as a new language, musical instrument, craft, or sport. Write a few lines as to how you'll accomplish this goal. Share your goal with a companion, and ask his or her support for achieving it.

Draw a picture illustrating the Book of Jonah. Use colorful markers or crayons to depict a scene that's especially meaningful for you. Then, write a few lines about its message for your own life. Get your children or grandchildren involved.

Read stories to your children about forgiveness, either from the Bible or from contemporary literature. Talk about what it means to forgive another and to accept forgiveness, and how hard it is to truly "let go." Invite them to talk about the conflicts they've had with others and to grant and seek forgiveness at this time of year.

Write about an episode this year in which you may have hurt someone by uttering unkind words, or failed to encourage or console when you had the opportunity. Then call or write this person and rectify this flaw. Ask if there's anything else you can do in a spirit of conciliation. Encourage your children to do the same.

Yom Kippur, a day of fasting, is also a time of purification. Discuss with your children and family members what it means to lead a pure life. Who exemplifies holiness or goodness in this or past eras? Talk about steps you and they plan to take to lead a holier life.

Do you or your family members have something in your home that you've borrowed or meant to return? Have you made a promise to someone that you haven't yet fulfilled? Talk about these issues and make plans to resolve them.

Let go of a grudge. Is there something from the past year about which you're bitter? Note it on a piece of paper, and then mark a large Hebrew letter *shin*, which begins the Hebrew word *shalom*, denoting peace and wholeness. Close your eyes and feel this emotion. With a sense of gratifying release, discard the paper.

REFLECTIONS

Sukkot

Sukkot ("Huts") reminds us that life is a spiritual journey. Just as the Israelites lived in desert shelters after fleeing Egypt, we erect temporary *sukkot* on this fall holiday as a reminder of their liberation. *Sukkot* is the third of the three pilgrimage holidays traditionally known as *regalim* (derived from *regel,* the Hebrew word for "foot" or "leg,"), for Jews in the Land of Israel trekked to Jerusalem on Passover, *Shavuot*, and *Sukkot*.

Sages have noted poetically that if Passover is about departures, recalling the Exodus from Egypt; and *Shavuot* is about arrivals, celebrating the Torah's bestowal at Mount Sinai; then *Sukkot* is the quintessential holiday of traveling, moving, and heading in the right direction. For more than 2,000 years, it was also a metaphor for the historical condition of the Jews, wandering homelessly across the globe.

Sukkot is mentioned specifically in the Bible:

> Three times a year you shall hold a festival for Me . . . the Feast of Ingathering at the end of the year, when you gather in the results of your work from the field. (Exodus 23:14–16)

On the 15th day of this seventh month is the Feast of Huts, seven days for the Lord. On the first day is a holy convocation; you shall not do any menial work. Seven days you shall bring a fire-offering to the Lord . . . When you have gathered in the income of the land, you shall take for yourselves on the first day the fruit of goodly trees, branches of palm trees, boughs of thick trees, and willows of the brook, and you shall rejoice before the Lord your God seven days.

For seven days you shall live in huts, every citizen in Israel shall dwell in huts, so that your generations know that I made the children of Israel dwell in huts when I brought them out from the Land of Egypt. (Leviticus 23:39–43)

This holiday's central symbol is the *sukkah*, a temporary structure of at least three walls and a roof composed of cut branches or leaves (*sechach*); it is carefully described in the Talmud and subsequent writings. For example, a *sukkah* must be less than 30 feet tall, the roof must offer more daytime shade than sunlight, and at night, the stars should be visible through its branches and leaves.

Traditionally Jews eat at least one meal daily in the *sukkah*, and along with friends and relatives, symbolically invite *ushpizin*, Judaism's spiritual founders to join: Abraham and Sarah, Isaac and Rebecca, Moses, Miriam, and David are some of the names invoked.

Also central to *Sukkot* is the ritual of the four species, reflecting the holiday's origins as a harvest and thanksgiving celebration. On each of *Sukkot's* eight days, we take four symbols of the earth's bounty: the *lulav* (a green, tri-species bouquet of palm frond, myrtle branch, and willow bough) and an *etrog* (a lemon-like fruit known as a citron). We shake them in six directions, as if we're showering the land with the dew of God's kindness. For Kabbalists, this deceptively small act is among Judaism's most powerful and transcendental holiday rituals, summoning and generating divine emanations throughout the world.

During the days of the Second Temple, *Sukkot* was a time of intense, ecstatic celebration. Dancing, torches, flutes, and juggling contributed to the revelry. Temple ceremonies also included water pouring, a ritual not mentioned in the Bible.

Because the *sukkah* is a symbol of transience, *Sukkot* is a time to identify what's temporary and ultimately trivial in your life—and conversely, what's enduring and significant. A good place to start with such soul-searching is your current dwelling: does it uplift you or give you a sense of spiritual well-being? If not, how can you make your home a greater place of Jewish vibrancy, such as through books, art and craftwork, greenery, and music? Take this opportunity to think and initiate action.

RECOMMENDED ACTIVITIES

Think of someone in Jewish history whom you admire—from biblical days to the present. He or she can be a hero or sage, scientist or writer, artist, musician, or political leader. Close your eyes, and inwardly invite this person into your *sukkah*. Is there a special question you'd like to ask? Then do so. You can also do this as a group activity. Perhaps place a picture of this person in your *sukkah*, or have your children draw pictures of their heroes to place on the walls of the *sukkah*.

Make a colorful box out of cardboard or wood to hold your *etrog*. Using colored crayons or markers, draw various nature symbols of your own design, such as the earth, fire, water, clouds, sun, and moon.

Stand comfortably in your *sukkah*. Think of a favorite dance of yours, and while you shake the *lulav* and *etrog* in the six directions, let your body sway joyfully in accordance with that dance.

Enjoy the foods of *Sukkot*: stuffed peppers, cabbage, or other vegetables, symbolizing a rich harvest, and fall fruits.

Children can make their own *Sukkot* dioramas out of shoeboxes, with the covers and one side removed. They can decorate the walls with harvest pictures, biblical scenes, or images of Jewish life. After they finish the interior, they can cover the top with twigs and greenery.

Inwardly invite a loved one or friend who is no longer alive into your *sukkah*. Close your eyes, and feel his or her warm familiar presence. As you recall how that person enriched your life, experience a sense of joy and contentment.

If you have a backyard, get together with friends and family to build a *sukkah*, either from scratch or with one of the many kits on the market. Invite children to make decorations that symbolize the harvest.

REFLECTIONS

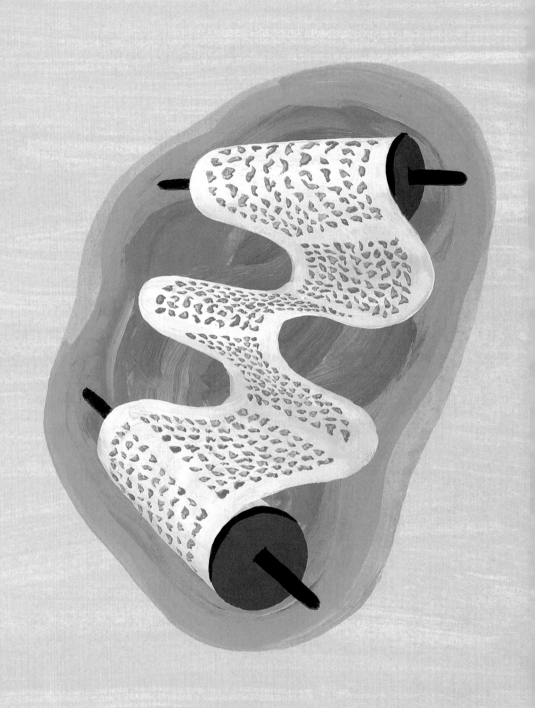

Shemini Atzeret & Simhat Torah

Simhat Torah (which means "rejoicing in the Torah") is a time of pure delight. In merry procession, we revel in the beloved presence of Torah in our lives, celebrating both the completion—and immediate beginning—of our annual cycle of readings from the Pentateuch.

Throughout history, Jews have truly been passionate about the Torah's ethical wisdom, spiritual guidance, and mystical rapture. As we come full circle, ending with Deuteronomy and beginning again with Genesis, our mood becomes joyful, but not merely in mind and spirit. By dancing with the Torah scrolls, we celebrate *physically* God's covenant with the Jewish people in a manner unmatched by any other festival. Tenderly, reverentially, ardently, and even ecstatically, our dance with the Torah fully involves our body and being.

Simhat Torah emerged as a special holiday comparatively late in Jewish history, in the tenth century C.E. In earlier Talmudic times, Jews observed the holiday merely as the second day of *Shemini Atzeret*, the festival that immediately follows the seven days of *Sukkot*. *Shemini Atzeret* was mandated as a quiet day of rest and refraining from work. During the era of the Second Temple, it became customary on *Shemini Atzeret* to pray for rain.

Originally, *Shemini Atzeret's* second day was observed in the Diaspora much as the first, albeit with different scriptural readings. But it soon became a distinctive holy day. Under the visionary leadership of the *geonim*—rabbinic scholars during the Babylonian Diaspora—an annual cycle for reading from the Torah became established among virtually all Jews. To reinforce this spiritual practice, the *geonim* developed the celebration of *Simhat Torah*, defining it as the completion of the one-year cycle of Torah reading with Moses' death at the end of Deuteronomy.

They also changed the *haftarah* reading, which had been a passage from I Kings 8, instead choosing the Book of Joshua, which continues the biblical narrative after Moses' death. Later, the *geonim* decided that the Torah-reading cycle shouldn't merely *end* on *Simhat Torah*, but should *begin* on this day as well, with the reading of Genesis 1.

Because each Torah portion of the week is traditionally regarded as bearing personal relevance for our own existence, the religious calendar—and our entire Jewish lifestyle—thus becomes cyclical, transcending the bounds and limits of linear time.

The festive *Simhat Torah* celebration begins the evening after *Shemini Atzeret's* first day. After *maariv*, the evening service, the congregation takes all of its Torah scrolls from the Ark, performing seven circlings *(hakkafot)* with them. In a grand march, the scrolls are carried by dancing congregrants around the raised pulpit area, the prayer hall, and sometimes even the building itself, with excursions into the streets. Everyone joins in the processions, often carrying flags with apples impaled on the flagpoles and a burning candle set into the apple; perhaps this fiery ritual relates to the burning torches the Levites used to juggle at the water-pouring celebrations in the Temple of Jerusalem.

According to Kabbalists, the seven *hakkafot* reflect and embody God's lower seven emanations *(sefirot)* of earthly existence: these encompass compassion and justice, aesthetic beauty, physical pleasure and ascetic denial, basic bodily vitality, and the natural world. The more we meditate on their mysterious qualities and essence, the greater our sense of inner fulfillment. On *Simhat Torah*, they suggest, we can feel all seven emanations cascading into divine Unity.

Recently *Simhat Torah* has become linked with new forms of dance and body movement as expressions of Jewish spirituality. Now is the time to rise above the trivialities of everyday existence, exulting physically in the Torah's splendor. Whatever your current stresses or challenges, hear *Simhat Torah's* call: dance and rejoice, for we have the Torah throughout our daily life.

RECOMMENDED ACTIVITIES

Select three verses from the Torah—such as from the Books of Psalms, Proverbs, or Ecclestiastes—that you find inspiring. Using colored pencils, markers, or crayons, write each verse on poster-size paper and mount it in your home. Invite your children to draw pictures inspired by these verses.

Choose one of the twenty-four books of the entire Torah and set a schedule to read it fully in the next month. Some books of the Torah, like Joel and Zechariah, are quite short and can be read easily in a few sittings. After you've completed the book, write a few lines on its meaning for you personally.

Select a verse from the Torah that seems to offer a relevant message for someone in your life. These can be words of encouragement, comfort, or inspiration. Make an attractive card with this verse and send it to that person.

Make a miniature scroll with your children, using small dowels and a roll of paper, and cover it with decorated fabric. Children can also create coverings for the miniature scrolls they receive in religious school as well as draw pictures of scenes from their favorite Bible stories.

Take a Hebrew Bible (if you don't own at least one version, now is definitely the time to purchase) and perform a new dance with it—such as a samba, mambo, swing, cha-cha, or tango. Play appropriate dance music in the background. The more who join you, the merrier.

If Jews are the People of the Book, think about what you can do to bring the joy of books into the lives of others. Get involved in a literacy project. Volunteer to read to new émigrés, the elderly, or disadvantaged youth.

REFLECTIONS

Hanukkah

Hanukkah, linked to the Hebrew root-word for "dedication," symbolizes faithful commitment to Jewish identity. Often called The Festival of Lights, the eight-day holiday is celebrated today with the lighting of candles, singing, parties, games, and gift-giving. The aroma of *latkes* (potato pancakes) fills the house as friends and families gather, lighting candles in the midst of winter's darkness.

Hanukkah is the only holiday for which Jews have a clear historical account of its origins. Yet it also ranks with *Simhat Torah* as one of only two festivals not mentioned in the Hebrew Bible, although the story from the apocryphal Book of Maccabees is included in some Christian Bibles. Yet it would be an exaggeration to say that *Hanukkah's* beginnings lack all mystery.

In its present form, *Hanukkah* dates back to 169 to 166 B.C.E., when the Maccabees—a family from the priestly tribe—led a struggle against the Greek overseers of the Land of Israel and against all Hellenized (Greek assimilated) Jews. Under the leadership of Matthias the Priest, a member of the Hasmonean family in the town of Modin, and his five sons, Jewish rebels successfully waged a fierce guerrilla war against the regular armies of Antiochus and his Jewish collaborators.

After their victory, the Hasmoneans entered the Holy Temple, which the Greeks had defiled with statues of their gods. After cleansing it, the Hasmoneans wished to kindle the menorah. Eventually, they found a single oil flask left undefiled, and miraculously, it lasted for eight days. In commemoration, the Hasmoneans legislated both the dates and regulations of the *Hanukkah* festival much as we know them today. The key ritual was to light an eight-pronged *hanukkiyah* (*Hanukkah* menorah), adding one candle per day at nightfall, accompanied by prayers and songs.

For almost two millennia, *Hanukkah* remained a definite but minor festival. Starting in the late nineteenth century, though, the holiday experienced a resurgence of interest in Central and Eastern Europe. The Maccabees' story suddenly became relevant to the growing number of Jews who were interested in reclaiming the Land of Israel as a modern political and/or religious state. To those who supported the pioneering and resettling efforts in the Holy Land, the story of *Hanukkah* had new resonance. Less important than the miracle of the oil flask that lasted for eight days, however, was the Maccabean courage, will, and resistance to assimilation.

Over the centuries, *Hanukkah* has generated a variety of customs, some decidedly more exalted than others. Because the Hebrew root of the word *Hanukkah* means "education" as well as "dedication," many Jewish communities globally have addressed educational issues publicly at this time of year. Jewish educational conferences are typically held, and some scholars trace the custom of giving children small cash amounts—*Hanukkah gelt* (Yiddish for "money")—to an effort to sweeten the process of Torah study.

More frivolous are the customs of gambling with cards or *dreidels* (spinning tops). Though the rabbis generally forbade gambling throughout the year, they relaxed this rule on *Hanukkah*, and Jews typically played for nuts rather than money. On each face of the *dreidel* is imprinted a single Hebrew letter: *nun, gimel, hay,* and *shin.* In Hebrew, they're said to stand for the phrase *Neis gadol ha-ya shom*: "A great miracle happened there." In Israel, instead of the letter *shin*, for "there," the *dreidel* will probably have a *pei*, beginning the Hebrew word *po*, which means "here."

In modern times, the ancient tradition of giving *Hanukkah gelt* to reward Torah study has evolved into the giving of small gifts each night. In Israel, a torchlight marathon takes place during *Hanukkah* from Modin, where Matthias first attacked Hellenistic idolatry, to Jerusalem. And, as a way to honor the oil of the Temple miracle, Jewish tradition has emphasized fried delicacies: in Eastern Europe, *latkes* or pancakes, and in Israel, *sufganiyot* or fried doughnuts.

Hasidism teaches that the religious dictum of kindling the *hanukkiyah*'s lights to make them visible from the street carries a larger, symbolic significance: each of our souls has a radiance that we need to bring out fully into the everyday world. Specifically, this means that every person has a unique essence of traits, talents, skills, and abilities that God has intended to share with others. Now is the time to reflect: What are your most precious and unique inner gifts? And how can you best share these with those important in your life?

Select a charity that's intrigued you, but to which you've never donated before. Using a dollar multiple of eight, representing the eight days of *Hanukkah*, make your financial contribution. Encourage your children to also choose a charity and contribute.

Write about a specific talent or skill that you have. Then describe how in the next year you can make it more visible and influential.

Make a *hanukkiyah* with a companion or child. As you gather the materials and create it, feel a sense of faith and historical Jewish connection. When you've built the *hanukkiyah*, recite the blessing known as the *Shehechiyanu*.

Since *Hanukkah* is a time of rededication, plan as a family to dedicate yourselves to a new mission, from helping out at a food pantry to assisting with a Jewish community project.

On each of the eight days of *Hanukkah*, think of a different person who has brought his or her unique light into your life. Then call or write this person, wishing a happy *Hanukkah*, and offering thanks for the radiance they've brought you.

REFLECTIONS

Tu B'Shevat

Tu B'Shevat ("the 15th day of the month of *Shevat*") is the birthday of fruit trees. Among modern Jews, this winter holiday is a time to celebrate the growth of all trees, and indeed of all nature, as well as the Land of Israel.

Known in the Talmud as the "New Year of the Trees," *Tu B'Shevat* has humble origins. It was originally a minor festival linked to the Torah commandment that Israelite farmers tithe their income to support the priesthood of the Temple of Jerusalem, the Levites who assisted them, and the poor.

Most likely, the date was marked for agricultural reasons. By the 15th of *Shevat* in the Land of Israel, the winter rains had mostly stopped and the old crop had been harvested. All fruit that ripened on and after that date was thus counted for tithing purposes as part of the *coming* year's crop; all fruit that ripened before the 15th of *Shevat* was considered part of the *previous* year's crop.

After the Second Temple's destruction in 70 C.E., Jewish agricultural tithing ceased. Initially surviving as a minor holiday, *Tu B'Shevat* involved fasting and penitential prayers. But the sacred songs of praise *(Hallel)* associated with festivals like *Rosh Hashanah* and *Sukkot* were not chanted, and the Talmud offered little commentary about holiday practices.

Over the centuries, *Tu B'Shevat* acquired a gentle celebratory quality. In the Jewish communities of Eastern and Central Europe, the custom arose of singing Psalm 104 and the fifteen Psalms of Ascent (Psalms 120–134) ascribed to the Levites as they mounted the fifteen steps into the inner court of the Temple of Jerusalem.

Along with these fifteen psalms went eating fifteen kinds of fruits, especially produce grown in the Land of Israel. *Tu B'Shevat* became associated with carob, a tree mentioned as the chief food eaten by the mystical, second century rabbi Simon ben Yochai while he hid for years from Roman soldiers. Other traditional fruits include dates, figs, grapes, olives, and pomegranates, all mentioned in the Torah as part of the Holy Land's bounty.

The Festival of Trees acquired a new importance in the nineteenth century, when Jewish pioneers in the Land of Israel found that planting trees was a crucial act of land restoration, making it possible to sow crops. As a result, settlers began encouraging their children to plant trees on *Tu B'Shevat*. Under the auspices of the Jewish National Fund, the holiday was singled out for fund-raising efforts to plant trees throughout the land.

Because Talmudic authorities didn't specify observances for *Tu B'Shevat*, the holiday has long been open to spiritual innovation. In the Israeli town of Safed, sixteenth-century Kabbalists created the *Tu B'Shevat seder*, a festive ritual meal in which four cups of wine and three types of fruit are consumed. Songs, especially about trees, are often interspersed with the wine and fruit, along with readings about trees from rabbinic sources, the *Midrash*, the *Zohar*, and modern Yiddish and Hebrew poets. Either at the beginning or end of the seder, some congregations plant trees in their communities or collect funds for trees in Israel.

The festival of *Tu B'Shevat* is an excellent time to feel and affirm your connection to nature, especially trees, long a key Jewish symbol and metaphor. Are you sufficiently linked to the natural world in your daily lifestyle? If not, what can you do to strengthen your linkage?

Not only is the mysterious divine structure of the cosmos known as the "Tree of Life," so, too, is the Torah itself. In the inspiring words of the Talmud, "Rabbi

Yohanan ben Zakkai said: 'If you're holding a seedling in your hand and you hear that the Messiah is coming, plant the seedling, and then go and greet the Messiah.'"

Take a bag of bread or cookie crumbs and go to a park or other outdoor space that's new to you. Feed the birds there. As you do so, think about your spiritual connection to nature, animals, and plants.

Using colored markers or crayons and a large piece of paper, draw a picture of a tree. Draw twenty-two branches, and on each branch, inscribe a Hebrew letter. Make this picture as colorful as possible and then hang it in your home. Invite your children to undertake this craft.

Plan a festive meal with different kinds of nuts and fruits. Choose at least one type of nut and one fruit that you've not eaten in some time. Invite guests to share this meal with you.

With your children, purchase seeds to plant in paper cups. When the seedlings grow, transplant them to decorative pots or outdoors in the springtime.

Plant a metaphorical seed in your life. This can involve a first lesson in a craft or skill, new language, or new field of study. Write a plan for how you will nurture this seed once you've planted it.

Be kind to the earth. Take steps to recycle or compost soil. Get your family or companions involved in a clean-up day in your community.

REFLECTIONS

Purim

Purim (which means "lots" or "sets" in Hebrew) intertwines mirth and merriment with the paradoxical theme of a God who often seems elusive. It is a time for carnivals, costume parties, satirical entertainment, noisemaking, and even religiously sanctioned drunkenness. Yet *Purim* has its dark side, reminding Jews of times of persecution, when God seemed hidden or hard to find.

The *Megillah* ("scroll") of Esther, which narrates the story of this holiday, is the only book of the Hebrew Bible that contains no divine name at all. In this sense, Kabbalists have explained, *Purim* is hardly just an appealing account of Jewish triumph over genocidal hatred. Rather, the *Megillah* of Esther is profoundly relevant for all our lives, bereft of direct divine revelation in the modern age.

In the biblical story, Esther, the Jewish wife of the Persian King Ahasuerus, and her cousin Mordechai outwit the evil prime minister Haman, who had issued an edict to exterminate all the kingdom's Jews.

According to tradition, this plot represented the most serious threat to Jewish existence in history, for virtually every Jew in the world lived within Ahasuerus's mighty dominion, and the king had initially approved Haman's edict.

But the plan was suddenly and miraculously turned on its head. Haman and his cohorts had used a lottery *(pur)* to select the specific pogrom date. However, just in the nick of time, the king was reminded of righteous Mordechai's past help in averting his own assassination. As a result, Haman and all his supporters were instead killed, and the Jews were elevated to great power and honor.

Aside from the possible existence of a Persian king resembling Ahasuerus, modern scholars insist that the *Purim* narrative lacks historical authenticity. They point out the striking correspondence of the names Mordechai and Esther to Marduk and Ishtar, two of the important ancient gods of the Near East. But whether the story happened exactly as described, or is an exaggerated version of an episode involving communal danger and triumph, *Purim* is an integral part of Judaism's festivities. Its spirit of revelry is conveyed in the famous Talmudic dictum that when the *Megillah* is chanted at synagogue, "It's the obligation of each person to be so drunk as not to be able to tell the difference between 'Blessed be Mordechai' and 'Cursed be Haman.'"

Traditionally, the holiday is preceded by a day of fasting. The festivities begin in the synagogue after sundown with the Megillah reading. Exuberant congregants, sometimes in costume, are armed with noisemakers *(graggers)*, which they shake boisterously whenever Haman's name is uttered. The rabbis and cantors, too, have fun with the holiday, dressing in costume and interspersing the liturgy with theatrics and whimsical melodies.

On *Purim,* it's also customary to send personally made gift baskets *(shalach manot)* involving food such as nuts, fruits, and *hamantaschen* (three-cornered pastries that recall Haman's three-cornered hat) to friends and also to give charitable donations to the poor. The holiday concludes at home in the late afternoon with a special meal involving friends and family.

Broadly, *Purim* is a happy—even raucous—time for affirming Jewish survival historically. On a personal level, it calls us to probe and ponder where the divine has entered our everyday life, and to celebrate that divine presence with laughter and delight. As you do so, look especially at seeming coincidences and synchronicities: those moments when the ordinary flow of time is re-channeled and new spiritual currents are born.

Create a *gragger* for use in the *Megillah* reading. It can be as simple as putting coins into an empty soda can or wooden box, or placing pebbles into a water bottle.

Make a *shalach manot* gift basket for a special person in your life. It can contain traditional items as well as a music CD or a book that this person will find gratifying.

Dress in an outlandish way: something you've never quite had the nerve to try. This can involve cosmetics, jewelry, accessories, or costumery. The wilder, the better.

With family or a group of friends, create skits or whimsical songs for a *Purim* celebration. Print lyrics so everybody can join in. Or set aside time for an evening of humorous readings.

Humor is a vital part of Jewish spirituality. Identify at least one way that you take yourself too seriously, and think how to inject more laughter into your weekly routine. It's helpful to ask at least two people who know you to help in this mirthful project.

REFLECTIONS

Passover

Passover (*"Pesach"* in Hebrew) commemorates the Exodus from Egypt, the Israelites' liberation from bondage to freedom led by Moses. It's a time of moving from oppression and darkness to God's protection and enlightenment. Perhaps the most widely celebrated of all the Jewish holidays, the festival has brought the Jewish people a great sense of shared identity, purpose, and community over the course of 3,500 years. As families and friends gather at the *seder* table, delighting in dishes prepared for generations, the meal is also punctuated with bittersweet reminders of more troubled times. On a personal level, Passover asks us to think about human freedom everywhere, and in our own daily lives.

Pesach takes its name from the Exodus narrative: During the tenth and ultimate plague inflicted on Pharaoh to break his will, God struck down the Egyptian firstborn, but the Israelites were spared. God *passed over* their dwellings, because Moses had instructed them to smear lamb's blood on their doorposts as a sign of their identity. That night, Pharaoh finally allowed the enslaved Israelites to depart his land, although he soon changed his mind and sent his army of chariots in hot pursuit. With Moses and his two siblings, Aaron and Miriam, at his side, the Jewish people crossed the parted Red Sea. Interestingly, some rabbis dispute the Red Sea translation and say it was a Sea of Reeds. Eventually they became a nation bound by a covenant with God and the Torah they received at Mount Sinai. Ever since the events of Exodus, Jews have gathered each year on the 15th of Sivan in joyful commemoration.

The *seder* (Hebrew for "order") is not simply a festive meal. It has a "script" or special prayerbook, the *Haggadah* (literally, "the Telling" in Hebrew), and today hundreds of *Haggadot* are available, ranging from traditional to feminist to vegetarian. Although the later sections of the traditional *Haggadah*, including folksongs, date back no more than 500 years, portions of the prayerbook were recited when the Second Temple still stood in Jerusalem.

Pesach involves more rituals than any other Jewish holiday—and more cleaning and cooking. Jews worldwide go through their homes to make them kosher or "fit" for the holiday and then prepare dishes that their great-grandparents enjoyed: *matzah* ball soup, *gefilte* (stuffed) fish, brisket, and potato *kugel* (a savory baked pudding). The primary rituals encompass three domains, all cited in Exodus:

> 1) Telling the story by means of the *seder.* "Remember this day, on which you went free from Egypt, the house of bondage, how the Lord freed you from it with a mighty hand..." (Exodus 13:3)
>
> 2) Eating *matzah* (unleavened bread): "At evening, you shall eat unleavened bread." (Exodus 12:18)
>
> 3) Refraining from eating or owning *hametz* (leavened bread or grain products): "On the very first day, you shall remove leaven from your house, for whosoever eats leavened bread from the first day to the seventh day, that person shall be cut off from Israel." (Exodus 12:15)

Traditionally, the *seder* has been a time for exuberant eating and singing; inviting friends, neighbors, and even strangers to participate; and mystically opening one's door to the Prophet Elijah. It's also a learning experience, deepening children's awareness, not only through the telling, but through such rituals as finding the hidden *matzah* portion known as the *afikomen* and receiving reward money, and reciting the Four Questions, which begin with the verse: "Why is this night different from all other nights?"

With the rise of Hasidism in eighteenth-century Eastern Europe, Passover acquired new significance. Its founders seized upon the *Haggadah's* inspiring dictum that "in every generation, each person should feel as though personally redeemed from Egypt."

Emphasizing that every Jewish holiday relates in a particular way to our individual "mission" (*tikkun*) in life, Hasidic leaders described *Pesach* as a metaphor for personal liberation: we each must free ourselves from that which enslaves us. For some, it might involve craving wealth or status, and for others, the trait of jealousy, impatience, or anger.

Among the Hasidim, the month of *Nisan* preceding Passover traditionally ranks with the month of *Elul* before *Rosh Hashanah* and *Yom Kippur* as a crucial time for self-reflection and spiritual guidance. In the weeks prior to *Pesach*, it was customary for Hasidim to journey often large distances, seeking their *rebbe's* (spiritual teacher's) blessing as well as his advice on how to apply the holiday's message to their own lives. In this way, the meticulous observance of Passover's many rituals was a joyful, and personally rewarding, task.

Consistent with the Kabbalistic and Hasidic perspective on *Pesach*, now is the time to ponder: What stifles, impedes, and thwarts your strongest impulses for inner well-being and transcendence? Is anything diminishing your sense of self-respect, dignity, and strength? If so, how can you free yourself? And, certainly with the help of others, how can you reach your own Promised Land?

In order to make the Four Questions fresh and alive, enlist three family members or friends. Each should choose one of the questions to write, in Hebrew if you can, on a piece of paper, writing the English below. Use a colorful crayon or marker. When all have finished, gather the four papers and paste them onto cardboard. Display it in your home during Passover.

Hasidism teaches that Passover is a time for self-reflection on the theme of slavery and freedom. Identify one thing in your life today that makes you feel enslaved or oppressed to some degree. Elicit friendly advice, and then plan how you will liberate yourself from this enslavement.

A number of communities are holding women's *seders* or alternative *seders*, usually not on the traditional *seder* night. Attend one. Are there rituals you can incorporate in your own *seder*?

Many new versions of the *Haggadah* are now available. Some may be more appealing to you than others, but all represent efforts to make the *Pesach* narrative relevant today. Select a *Haggadah* you've never used before, and make it at least an adjunct—if not the primary guide—for your *seders*.

The *mitzvah* of hospitality is especially important on this holiday. Invite a new acquaintance, or even a stranger to your *seder*, perhaps a friend's friend or relative. Make your guest feel honored and appreciated.

Invite your children to draw pictures based on the Passover story.

Purchase a CD, audiocassette, or sheet music of the Passover melodies. Play them as the week approaches to get into the spirit.

REFLECTIONS

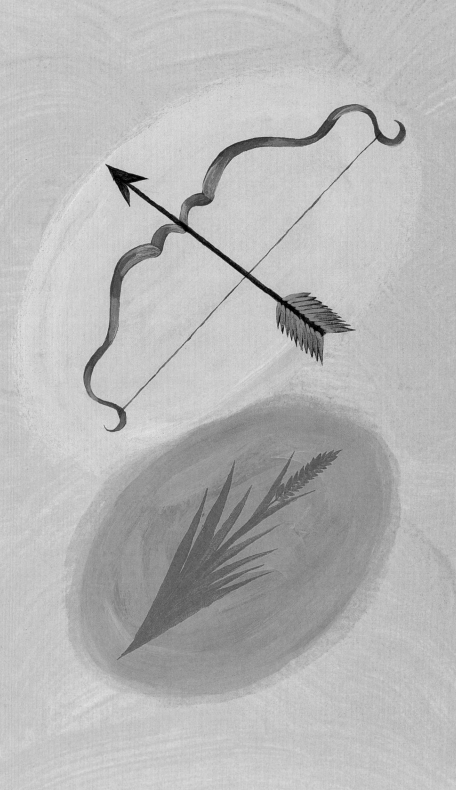

Lag B'Omer

With its ancient symbol of the bow representing both archery and a heavenly rainbow, *Lag B'Omer*'s theme is of spring festivity and Jewish spiritual renewal. Its name literally means the 33rd day in the counting of the *omer* ("sheaf of barley"), so called because the two Hebrew letters in *Lag, lamed* and *gimel*, signify the number 33.

Mandated in the Five Books of Moses, the counting of the *omer*, an ancient agricultural practice related to the harvesting of grain, begins on the second night of Passover and takes place each day during the forty-nine-day period until the festival of *Shavuot*. At the start of this sacred interval, the Torah prescribed waving the *omer* in a special ritual at the Temple of Jerusalem, and then on the 50th and final day, bringing two loaves of wheat to be waved as an additional Temple offering.

After the Temple was destroyed in 70 c.e., the sages replaced the agricultural emphasis of the *omer*-counting with one of limited mourning, for no longer could Jews adhere to the religious obligation of Temple offerings.

Precisely how *Lag B'Omer* (which falls on the 18th day of the month of *Iyar*) became a festive day exempted from this mourning is steeped in folklore. Interestingly, all of these legends focus on the second century c.e., when the Romans brutally destroyed the remaining features of Jewish statehood but were unable to extinguish Jews spiritually.

A popular legend is that on the 33rd day of the *omer*-counting period, a plague that had decimated Rabbi Akiba's thousands of ardent followers mysteriously ended. A related legend is that on this day Rabbi Akiba defied the Roman edict against Torah study, an act punishable by torture and death. Gathering a group of his adherents, he disguised their plan to study Torah in the wilderness by arming everyone with bows and arrows, as though these scholars were hunting for game like their Roman oppressors.

According to still another cluster of legends, on *Lag B'Omer* in the year 148 c.e., Simon ben Yochai, the chief mystical disciple of Rabbi Akiba, emerged triumphantly from the caves in which he and his son Eliezer had hidden from Roman soldiery for more than a decade. Ben Yochai is revered by traditionalists as the true originator of the sacred *Zohar*, the book of mystical teachings that first appeared in thirteenth century Spain. His devotion to Torah study in the face of unrelenting persecution has made him a heroic figure.

For many centuries, ben Yochai's gravesite in the Israeli town of Meron, near Safed, has been the site of *Lag B'Omer* pilgrimages for Hasidism and other mystical Jews. They celebrate his righteous life by lighting bonfires, dancing, singing, and feasting. The custom began with the sixteenth-century Kabbalist Rabbi Chaim Vital. His spiritual circle also interpreted the bow given to children on *Lag B'Omer* as symbolic of the rainbow (the same Hebrew word is used for both) that will light up the heavens on the messianic day of redemption.

On *Lag B'Omer*, it's also customary for Israeli parents to bring their three-year-old sons to Meron for their first haircuts, while in the Diaspora, Orthodox families often hold haircutting ceremonies on this day. Reflecting the Talmudic view that this chronological age marks the end of infancy and the start of childhood religious training and awareness, this holiday ritual also derives from the *midrash* that Isaac—the first child to be Jewish from birth—was weaned by his mother, Sarah, on his third birthday.

For Jews living outside of Israel, *Lag B'Omer* is a festive day, particularly among schoolchildren, with hikes in the woods, picnics, and playful archery. Because weddings and public concerts are prohibited on virtually all other days in the *omer-* counting period between Passover and *Shavuot*, it's become a popular occasion for such family and communal celebrations.

Traditionally, the ancient Jewish wisdom text known as *Pirke Avot* ("Ethics of the Fathers") is studied during this forty-nine-day interval. Because of its homage to Simon ben Yochai, *Lag B'Omer* is a particularly auspicious time to ponder *Pirke*'s aphorisms about our souls' purpose, destiny, and fulfillment. Among its most famous guideposts are the three rhetorical questions posed by the sage Hillel: "If I am not for myself, who will be?"; "If I am only for myself, what am I?"; "And, if not now, when?"

On a large piece of paper, write the letters *lamed* and *gimel*. In Jewish tradition, the letter *lamed* symbolizes learning and the letter *gimel* represents synthesizing or integrating seeming opposites. As you gaze at them, think what you can do to bring these qualities more fully into your life.

The world today is plagued not only by illness, but by negativities such as illiteracy, poverty, despair, cynicism, intolerance, and conflict. Identify one such plague and write a few sentences on how you can help to stem its tide. Get involved in a *mitzvah* project, either individually, with your family, or through the synagogue or community.

Sit in a relaxed position, and free from distractions, list forty-nine blessings in your present life. These can be individuals, favorite activities, and aspects that you normally take for granted, such as physical health and financial stability. Feel a sense of gratitude as you name each blessing in writing. Engage your children in this task.

Hold a picnic or outdoor celebration with family members, friends, or neighbors.

Take a long, leisurely walk in a park or natural setting that you haven't visited for a while. Spend at least one hour on this walk, and invite a companion. Choose a spiritual topic to discuss, such as how to show greater gratitude, compassion, or forgiveness toward others.

REFLECTIONS

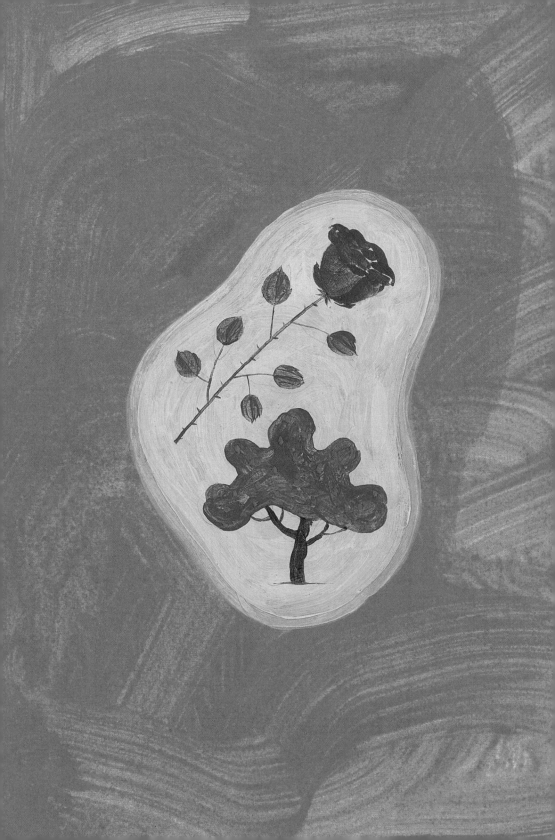

Shavuot

Held exactly seven weeks after Passover's second day, *Shavuot* (which means "Weeks") marks divine revelation. This spring holiday celebrates the awesome time when all Jews stood at Mount Sinai and received the Torah from God.

Although it may be the least known of the three pilgrimage festivals (the others are *Sukkot* and Passover), today *Shavuot* is gaining renewed interest, especially among those drawn to Judaism's mystical side. It is a time of all-night study of Jewish texts and religious-school celebrations, as well as a time to welcome converts and read the story of Judaism's best-known convert in the Book of Ruth.

Like many Jewish holidays, *Shavuot* has undergone major change over the millennia. Nowhere in the Bible itself is any link made between the Revelation at Sinai and a particular commemorative day. Originally an agricultural festival, *Shavuot* marked the forty-ninth day of the counting of the *omer* (sheaf of barley), when wheat was ready to be harvested.

Originally, *Shavuot* had no fixed date. It was simply a one-day festival during which two loaves of leavened bread were brought to the Temple as an offering of thanks. It also marked a new agricultural season, when the first fruits of the land were brought to the Temple.

After the Second Temple was destroyed in 70 C.E., the focus of *Shavuot* changed significantly, as Jews could no longer observe the agricultural rites in the Temple. Instead, over the ensuing centuries, the Talmudic sages began associating *Shavuot* with God's bestowing the Torah on the Jewish people. With the fixing of the Hebrew calendar, the holiday's date permanently became the 6th day of the month of Sivan. Diaspora Jews developed the custom of celebrating the holiday for two days.

Lacking a specific ritual, *Shavuot* has few distinctive practices. Yet over the centuries, a variety of customs have arisen, including decorating the home and synagogue with green plants, branches, and even trees. Symbolically, the Torah has always been known as a "Tree of Life" as it provides spiritual vitality.

Shavuot's special flower is the rose because of a play on words in the Book of Esther (Esther and her cousin Mordechai came from the Persian town of Sushan, and the Hebrew word for rose is *shoshan*). Cut-paper decorations of trees and flowers, particularly roses, have long been popular on this holiday, and Jews adorn synagogues and homes with these embellishments.

It's also customary to eat dairy foods, including blintzes and cheesecake, on *Shavuot*. According to legend, when the Israelites received the laws of *kashrut* (kosher practices) at Sinai, they realized that not all their cooking pots were kosher, so they ate uncooked dairy foods instead. Another view compares the sweetness of Torah to "milk and honey."

Shavuot's second day is known as the festival of *matnat yad* ("the day of giving") and we recite a special prayer on behalf of those who contribute to charity.

The Sabbath preceding *Shavuot* is called *Shabbat Kallah*, the name typically given to a Sabbath before a wedding. But in this case, the marriage or Covenant is between the Jewish people and God. On this Sabbath, it's customary to read the Book of Ruth, with its tender love story of Ruth's conversion to Judaism underlining this spiritual theme. Among some Jews, the Book of Ruth's first half is also read on *Shavuot*'s opening day and concluded on its second day.

According to Kabbalists, the divine voice emanates ceaselessly from Mount Sinai: *Shavuot* reminds us to heed revelation's call in seemingly ordinary events. It's a time to reflect on the most important moments of your life, the "peaks" of joy and meaning, and to ponder: How can I best honor and integrate these into my daily realm of work and relationships? How can I be more fully open to the Voice at Sinai?

RECOMMENDED ACTIVITIES

Identify a revelation in your own life: a moment of soulful awakening and joy. If no single incident stands out, then think of one experience this past year that held "peak" qualities for you. What triggered this experience? How did you feel? How has it changed your view of life?

Select a dairy food that you've never eaten before, or haven't in a long time, such as a special cheese or yogurt. Share it with a companion. Or prepare cheese blintzes or a noodle pudding *(kugel)* with friends or children.

With children, create a decorative platter with seven seasonal fruits, a number with mystical significance in Judaism. When you eat a fruit for the first time this season, recite the *Shehechiyanu*, the Hebrew prayer said when doing something for the first time.

Invite two or more people to join you at night to study a Jewish text. It can be from the Torah or Kabbalah, or perhaps a Hasidic tale. Be sure that each person answers this question: how does the text relate to our personal lives today?

The sages have always regarded Hebrew as a sacred language, a medium of revelation. Allowing yourself ample time to make this a meditative experience, draw each of the twenty-two Hebrew letters on a large sheet of paper. Be as artistic and stylish as you like. In producing each letter, feel its divine energy exalting you.

REFLECTIONS

Tisha B'Av

While most Jewish holidays are times of celebration, the theme of *Tisha B'Av* ("the 9th day of the month of *Av* ") is one of mourning for the destruction of both the First and Second Temples of Jerusalem. Held in the middle of the summer, *Tisha B'Av* is the most difficult fast on the Jewish calendar and perhaps the bleakest time, as it is preceded by three weeks of intensifying restrictions in observant communities. Yet it is also a time of personal and communal faith—encompassing hope and optimism—that Jews will witness an age "when nation shall not make war upon nation" and "swords shall be made into ploughshares."

When the First Temple was destroyed in 586 B.C.E. by order of the Babylonian King Nebuchadnezzar, the Jews went into exile and began observing an annual period of fasting in memory of the Temple's destruction. When the Babylonian exile ended and Jews returned to the Land of Israel, reconsecrating the Temple around 515 C.E., they preserved *Tisha B'Av* as a day of mourning, even though the Prophet Zechariah decreed that it could become a festival of joy.

But in 70 C.E., the Second Temple was destroyed by order of Vespasian, a general of the Roman Empire. The actual event occurred on the 10th of *Av*, marking the beginning of the Diaspora. Though Jewish leaders tried for more than sixty years to regain political and religious control of the Holy Land from the Romans, they never succeeded.

Indeed, after the disastrous military revolt led by the Jewish general Bar Kochba ("Son of the Star") from 132–135 C.E., the Romans forbade Torah teaching, Sabbath observance, and circumcision, naming them capital offenses. Thousands were sold into slavery. Jerusalem was rebuilt as Aelia Capitolina and no Jew was allowed within its gates. The emperor renamed the country Palestine ("Land of the Philistines"), a label deliberately chosen to indicate that the territory was no longer considered Judean. According to tradition, it was also on *Av*'s 9th day that the Romans captured the city of Bethar, the last stronghold of Bar Kochba's revolt, and exactly a year later, ploughed under the entire Temple site.

Seeking to legitimize *Tisha B'Av* as a major holiday, the Talmudic sages looked back into Jewish history. They determined that on this date the fearful Israelites refused to enter the Holy Land after their liberation from Egyptian bondage. As the Israelites lamented their decision to leave captivity, God not only commanded them to wander the desert for forty years until the entire generation died, but declared: "You have wept without cause; therefore I will set [this day] for a weeping throughout the generations to come."

Still later, other historical calamities became associated with *Tisha B'Av*, including the Jewish expulsion from England in 1290, and even more disastrously, from Spain in 1492.

Although *Tisha B'Av* stands alongside *Yom Kippur* as one of Judaism's two major fast days, its mournful mood sharply differs from the somber but lofty self-examination mandated on the Day of Atonement. While the Torah scrolls are cloaked in white at *Yom Kippur*, at *Tisha B'Av* the Ark of the Torah is draped in black or left open and empty, stripped of its holy scrolls. There are no bright lights, only candles casting a dim and flickering glow. In some Sephardic and Far Eastern congregations, even these candles are put out near the close of the service, so that it ends in complete darkness. As is customary for mourners, congregants sit on the floor, or on low benches and cushions. Worshippers study only the sad passages of the Bible and

Talmud, such as the Book of Lamentations, Job, the grieving sections of Jeremiah's prophecies, and the commentaries based on them.

While the sundown and morning services are mournful, the spirit of the *minchah* (afternoon service) is hopeful and redemptive. Among the Sephardim, women have traditionally worn perfume to symbolically welcome the Messiah. Immediately after sundown, Jews break the fast together, and after washing their faces, go outside to perform the joyful service of *kiddush levana*: hallowing the moon. Although this service may be performed when the crescent moon is visible in the first half of any month, many Jewish communities specifically connect it with the ending of *Tisha B'Av*.

For some Jews today, the 9th of *Av* is linked via the calendar to the atomic bombs dropped on Hiroshima and Nagasaki in August 1945. Contemporary *Tisha B'Av* commemorations may include discussions on war, human violence, and suffering— and the ancient prophetic call for universal peace and justice.

On *Tisha B'Av*, it's vital to think about what we can do individually, and as part of a Jewish community, to actualize the prophets' stirring dreams and visions. In our souls, homes, towns, cities, nations, and continents, what propensity for hatred and violence still exists? And how can we eliminate this potential and replace it with our energies for love, spirituality, and enlightenment?

Think of someone in your life who has recently been physically ill, incapacitated, or highly stressed. What can you do, individually or as a family, to ease the burden? Gently refuse all offers of reciprocation.

Recall a painful event in your life and identify the "silver lining" that you now can see—perhaps a valuable lesson you learned from the experience. What advice would you give someone struggling today with a similar event? Write a few sentences. If you are struggling with bereavement, consider joining a group in which you can work out some of your grief.

Identify a social problem in your community, such as homelessness, illiteracy, or the lack of recreational facilities for teens. In a few sentences, describe your plan to help, such as donating your time as a hands-on volunteer, raising funds, or joining a letter-writing campaign. Become part of a social-action group, either through your congregation or another community organization, or consider starting one.

Because *Tisha B'Av* falls in the summer, when children are not in religious school, its lessons are often not conveyed. Use this occasion to talk about the destruction of the First and Second Temples, and other calamities that befell the Jews at this time of year. Create pictures or a diorama of the Temple. In keeping with the theme of the "silver lining," move on to the positive things that have arisen out of the ashes of destruction. These can also be drawn.

Tisha B'Av involves three Hebrew letters: *tet* (for *Tisha*, representing the number nine), and the letters *alef* and *bet*, whose two letters spell the month of *Av*. Using a black crayon or marker, draw these three letters onto a large paper. Now, take a colored crayon or marker, and encircle the letters with a rainbow, the traditional Jewish symbol of hope and redemption. This is a good project to do as a family.

Read Psalm 137 as a family or in a study group, which exhorts us to remember Jerusalem: "If I forget thee, O Jerusalem, let my right hand wither." Discuss what Jerusalem means to you personally, symbolically, and as a holy city. If you've been to Jerusalem and the Wall, talk about its impact on you or draw pictures.

REFLECTIONS

The Jewish Holiday Calendar

The "modern" Hebrew calendar, a lunar calendar, was devised more than 2,000 years ago. It's tuned to the moon's rotation around the earth, which takes 29.5 days. Each Hebrew month is counted as either twenty-nine or thirty days. Twelve of these months make one year.

This setup causes a problem in reconciliation, for twelve lunar months add up to approximately 354 days, which is eleven days short of a solar year. Therefore, if we didn't adjust the Hebrew calendar to match the solar calendar, *Rosh Hashanah* and all the other Jewish holidays would wander around the solar year. In one year they might fall in winter, and a few years later, in summer. Because several holidays celebrate harvests and are tied to the Land of Israel's seasons, that would generate an awkward situation. For instance, it would seem absurd to celebrate the fall harvest *(Sukkot)* in early spring.

To solve this problem, the sages created a leap year containing an entire additional month—known as *Adar Bet* (that is, a second month of *Adar*), which is inserted occasionally after the regular late-winter month of *Adar*.

To align regularly with the solar year, the Hebrew leap year occurs seven times within a nineteen-year cycle; this averages out to about one leap year every two or three solar years. As a result, in any given Hebrew year, a Jewish holiday may occur "early" or "late" in relation to the secular calendar. For example, in some solar years, *Rosh Hashanah* may fall "early," at the beginning of September, and in others, as "late" as early October.

Each Jewish holiday always begins at sunset on the *previous* day of the secular calendar. For instance, the Sabbath always begins at sunset on Friday.

HEBREW MONTH	AUGUSTAN CALENDAR
Tishri	September/October
Heshvan	October/November
Kislev	November/December
Tevet	December/January
Shevat	January/February
Adar I	February/March
Adar II	February/March
Nisan	March/April
Iyar	April/May
Sivan	May/June
Tammuz	June/July
Av	July/August
Elul	August/September

ROSH HODESH The Festival of the New Moon

CALENDAR DATE: In both the Land of Israel and the Diaspora, Jews celebrate *Rosh Hodesh* on the first day of each Hebrew month.

OBSERVANCE VARIABILITY: All Jews observe for one day.

ROSH HASHANAH

CALENDAR DATE: 1–2 *Tishri* (usually early September through early October)

OBSERVANCE VARIABILITY: In both Israel and the Diaspora, observance lasts two days, except among Reform and Reconstructionist Jews, who observe only the first day.

YOM KIPPUR

CALENDAR DATE: 10 *Tishri* (usually mid-September through mid-October)

OBSERVANCE VARIABILITY: All Jews observe for one day.

SUKKOT

CALENDAR DATE: 15–21 *Tishri* (usually late September through late October)

OBSERVANCE VARIABILITY: Traditionally, *Sukkot* is observed for seven days. In the Diaspora, the first two are full festival days, when work and travel are prohibited; the third through sixth are "intermediate" days (known generically as *Chol Hamoed*), when work and travel are permitted; and the seventh day (known as *Hoshana Rabbah*) is almost completely festive. In Israel and among Reform and Reconstructionist Jews in the Diaspora, the first day is a full festival day, the second through sixth are "intermediate," and the seventh is likewise *Hoshana Rabbah*.

SIMHAT TORAH

CALENDAR DATE: 22–23 *Tishri* (usually early through late October)

OBSERVANCE VARIABILITY: In the Diaspora, where *Shemini Atzeret* is traditionally observed for two days, 22 *Tishri* is celebrated as *Shemini Atzeret* and 23 *Tishri* as *Simhat Torah*. In Israel and among Reform and Reconstructionist Jews, all the rituals of both holidays take place on 22 *Tishri*.

HANUKKAH

CALENDAR DATE: 25 *Kislev*–2 *Tevet* (usually late November through late December)

OBSERVANCE VARIABILITY: All Jews observe for eight days. Among Hasidim, the eighth day is especially festive with meals and celebrations.

TU B'SHEVAT

CALENDAR DATE: 15 *Shevat* (usually late January through mid-February)

OBSERVANCE VARIABILITY: All Jews observe for one day.

PURIM

CALENDAR DATE: 14 *Adar* (usually late February through late March)

OBSERVANCE VARIABILITY: All Jews observe for one day. Traditionally, *Purim* is preceded by a day of fasting on 13 *Adar*, known as the Fast of Esther, in remembrance of the three-day fast the Jews of Persia initiated at Esther's request. In accordance with the Talmudic sages, *Purim* in Jerusalem is instead observed on 15 *Adar*.

PASSOVER

CALENDAR DATE: 15–21/22 *Nisan* (usually late March through late April)

OBSERVANCE VARIABILITY: In the Diaspora, Passover is traditionally observed for eight days; the first two and last two are full festival days and the third through seventh are "intermediate" *(Chol Hamoed)*. In Israel and among Reform and Reconstructionist Jews in the Diaspora, Passover is celebrated for seven days. The first and seventh are full festival days, and the other days are "intermediate." Traditionally, the day before Passover is a fast day for firstborn. Known as *Ta'Anit Bekhorim*, it's also observed by some who are not firstborn but choose to fast out of religious devotion.

LAG B'OMER

CALENDAR DATE: 18 *Iyar* (usually late April through late May)

OBSERVANCE VARIABILITY: All Jews observe for one day.

SHAVUOT

CALENDAR DATE: 6–7 *Sivan* (usually late May through mid-June)

OBSERVANCE VARIABILITY: All Jews observe *Shavuot* on 6 *Sivan*. In the Diaspora, it's traditionally observed on 7 *Sivan* as well.

TISHA B'AV

CALENDAR DATE: 9 *Av* (usually in mid-July through mid-August)

OBSERVANCE VARIABILITY: All Jews observe for one day.

Glossary

Afikomen: portion of the *matzah* that's hidden during the *seder,* found during a hunt, and then ransomed.

Amidah: the central portion of all services.

Baal Shem Tov: "Master of the Good Name," the popular appellation of Israel ben Eliezer (c. 1698–1760) the charismatic founder of Hasidism.

Berakhah: a blessing.

Besht: an abbreviation of the Hebrew name Baal Shem Tov.

Birkhat Hamazon: the blessing after the meal.

Chag: festival day.

Chol Hamoed: ordinary or intermediate days of a festival—days in the middle of Passover or *Sukkot* when work is allowed.

Daven: to pray.

Diaspora: the forced exile of the Jewish people since the destruction of the Second Temple of Jerusalem, used today as a term for Jewish communities outside Israel.

Gemara: (Aramaic) literally "to study." It is the commentary surrounding the Mishnah. The Gemara and Mishnah together comprise the Talmud.

Geonim: rabbinic scholars of the Babylonian Diaspora.

Haftarah: a passage from the Prophets read on a given Sabbath or festival.

Haggadah: the *seder* prayerbook, which tells the story of the Exodus.

Halakhah: Jewish law.

Hallah: the traditional braided bread eaten on *Shabbat* and other festive occasions.

Hametz: leavened bread or grain products, forbidden at Passover.

Hasidism: the popular, charismatic movement that arose among East European Jewry in the late eighteenth century. *Hasid* means "pious" in Hebrew.

Havdalah: the ritual marking the end of the Sabbath and holidays.

Havurah: a group of friends who get together to study Jewish texts, gather for *Shabbat* and holidays, and perhaps do *mitzvot.*

Kabbalah: from the Hebrew root-word "to receive," is often used as a generic term for Jewish mysticism per se; it more precisely refers to esoteric thought from the late-twelfth-century onward.

Kaddish: a prayer recited at various points in the liturgy. One version is recited by mourners.

Kavana: intentionality, said of heartfelt prayer or devotion.

Kiddush: the sanctification of the day, recited over wine at the start of festivals and the Sabbath.

Maariv: evening prayer service.

Machzor: prayerbook for *Rosh Hashanah* and *Yom Kippur*, and sometimes other festivals.

Midrash: the legendary tradition of Judaism. A *midrash*, lowercased, (with the plural *midrashim*) is a specific Midrash legend.

Minchah: afternoon prayer service.

Mishnah: the earliest, post-biblical text of Jewish law and belief. It consists of six orders, each divided into three tractates. It is believed to have been completed in the early third century C.E.

Mitzvah: commandment from God; more broadly, a good deed.

Sefirot: the emanations or manifestations of earthly existence and the divine, represented as a Tree of Life in the mystical tradition of Kabbalah. Kabbalists speak about ten *sefirot*, with the lower seven being the earthly ones.

Shaharit: morning prayer service.

Shehechiyanu: the traditional blessing to express gratitude for a joyful event in our life.
In Hebrew transliteration: *Baruch Ata Adonai, Eloheynu Melech Ha-olam shehechiyanu v'keyamanu v'higianu lazman hazeh.*
In English translation: Blessed are You, Ruler of the Universe, You have kept us alive, and sustained us, and enabled us to reach this moment.

Shekhinah: the indwelling of God, associated with radiance and joy, in our earthly existence; also the feminine manifestation of God, exemplified symbolically by the "Sabbath Queen."

Shul: synagogue.

Siddur: prayerbook.

Talmud: the summary of the Judaic oral tradition, compiled and written down by sages in the Land of Israel and Babylonia. Completed about 500 C.E., it exists in two editions, one for each center of world Judaism of the time. The Babylonian edition is by far the more comprehensive and authoritative version. The Talmud comprises the Mishnah and Gemara.

Tashlikh: a ceremony held on *Rosh Hashanah* involving the symbolic casting away of sins by throwing breadcrumbs or stones into water.

Teshuvah: repentance, or more broadly, return and ascent to one's divine source of origin.

Tzedakah: charity.

Torah: in a narrow sense, the Pentateuch. More generally, Torah is understood to comprise the twenty-four books of the Bible and the Talmud.

Yom tov: a festival.

Zohar: the major mystical work of Judaism, which first appeared in thirteenth-century Spain.

RESOURCES

The Aryeh Kaplan Reader. Brooklyn, New York: Mesorah, 1983.

Cardin, Nina Beth. *The Tapestry of Jewish Time: A Spiritual Guide to Holidays and Life-Cycle Events.* New York: Behrman House, 2000.

Central Conference of American Rabbis. *Gates of the Seasons, A Guide to the Jewish Year.* Edited by Peter S. Knobel. New York: Central Conference of American Rabbis, 1983.

Cuyler, Margery. *Jewish Holidays.* Illustrated by Lisa C. Wesson. New York: Holt, Rinehart and Winston, 1978.

Donin, Hayim Halevy. *To Be a Jew: A Guide to Jewish Observance in Contemporary Life.* New York: Basic Books, 1972.

Epstein, Morris. *All About Jewish Holidays and Customs,* revised edition. New York: Ktav, 1970.

Greenberg, Blu. *How to Run a Traditional Jewish Household.* New York: Simon and Schuster, 1983.

Heschel, Abraham Joshua. *The Sabbath: Its Meaning for Modern Man.* New York: Farrar, Straus & Giroux, 1951.

Hoffman, Edward (Editor). *Opening the Inner Gates: New Paths in Kabbalah and Psychology,* 2nd edition. Commack, New York: Four Worlds Press, 1998.

Hoffman, Edward. *The Heavenly Ladder: Kabbalistic Techniques for Inner Growth.* Commack, New York: Four Worlds Press, 1998.

Isaacs, Ronald H. *Words for the Soul: Jewish Wisdom for Life's Journey.* Northvale, New Jersey: Aronson, 1996.

Kook, Abraham Isaac. *The Lights of Penitence, Lights of Holiness, the Moral Principles, Essays, Letters, and Poems.* Translation and introduction by Ben-Zion Bokser. New York: Paulist Press, 1978.

Newman, Louis. *Hasidic Anthology.* New York: Schocken, 1975.

Schauss, Hayyim. *The Jewish Festivals, History and Observance.* Translated by
Samuel Jaffe. New York: Schocken, 1974.

Schneerson, Menachem M. *Timeless Patterns in Time: Chassidic Insights into the
Cycle of the Jewish Year.* Brooklyn, New York: Kehot Publication Society, 1993.

Strassfeld, Michael. *The Jewish Holidays: A Guide and Commentary.* New York:
HarperCollins, 1985.

Trepp, Leo. *The Complete Book of Jewish Observance.* New York: Behrman House,
1980.

Waskow, Arthur. *Seasons of our Joy.* Boston: Beacon, 1982.